Minecraft and STEAM

Patterns and Numbers in Minecraft

Adam Hellebuyck and **Michael Medvinsky**

CHERRY LAKE
Publishing

Published in the United States of America by Cherry Lake Publishing
Ann Arbor, Michigan
www.cherrylakepublishing.com

Reading Adviser: Marla Conn, MS, Ed, Literacy Specialist, Read-Ability, Inc.

Photo Credits: © Adam Hellebuyck and Michael Medvinsky/Cover, 1, 7, 8, 19, 24; ©Wesley Fryer/flickr, 5, 16;
© Augustas Cetkauskas/Shutterstock.com, 9; © Sebastian Draxler/flickr, 11; © Pressmaster/Shutterstock.com 13;
© M.Halichev/Shutterstock.com, 15; © Elpisterra/Shutterstock.com, 17; ©Mike Prosser/flickr, 18; © Anamaria Mejia/
Shutterstock.com, 21; © sirtravelalot/Shutterstock.com, 23; © wavebreakmedia/Shutterstock.com, 25; © Cultura
Motion/Shutterstock.com, 26; © Bananinha God/flickr, 29

Graphic Element Credits: © Ohn Mar/Shutterstock.com, back cover, multiple interior pages; © Dmitrieva Katerina/
Shutterstock.com, back cover, multiple interior pages; © advent/Shutterstock.com, back cover, front cover, multiple interior
pages; © Visual Generation/Shutterstock.com, multiple interior pages; © anfisa focusova/Shutterstock.com, front cover,
multiple interior pages; © Babich Alexander/Shutterstock.com, back cover, front cover, multiple interior pages;

Library of Congress Cataloging-in-Publication Data

Names: Hellebuyck, Adam, author. | Medvinsky, Michael, author.
Title: Patterns and numbers in Minecraft: Math / by Adam Hellebuyck and Michael
    Medvinsky.
Description: Ann Arbor, MI : Cherry Lake Publishing, [2019] | Series:
    Minecraft and STEAM | Audience: Grades 4 to 6. | Includes bibliographical
    references and index.
Identifiers: LCCN 2018035563| ISBN 9781534143166 (hardcover) | ISBN
    9781534139725 (pbk.) | ISBN 9781534140929 (pdf) | ISBN 9781534142121
    (hosted ebook)
Subjects: LCSH: Geometry—Juvenile literature. | Mathematics—Juvenile
    literature. | Architecture—Computer simulation—Juvenile literature. |
    Minecraft (Game)—Juvenile literature.
Classification: LCC QA445.5.H4425 2019 | DDC 794.8/5—dc23
LC record available at https://lccn.loc.gov/2018035563

Printed in the United States of America
Corporate Graphics

Table of Contents

INTRODUCTION

One of the most exciting parts of *Minecraft* is that you can build anywhere and in any way you want. It can be fun to build **spontaneously** with whatever blocks you have in your inventory. It can also be exciting to plan your creations in advance. When you plan in advance, you can use math to create beautiful structures. Let's take a closer look and discover how!

You can build amazing, out-of-this-world designs by planning your creations and using math!

CHAPTER ONE

Geometry: Simple Shapes

In the real world, you may have noticed that most buildings are usually built using a combination of shapes. The study of these shapes is called **geometry**. For instance, a simple house is really just a combination of two to three different shapes: a rectangle or square and a triangle. Beam bridges, the oldest and simplest type of bridges, are built using vertical and horizontal

In the three-dimensional (3D) *Minecraft* world, you can determine where you are using **coordinates**. The X coordinate shows your longitude, the distance to the east or west from where you are. The Z coordinate shows your latitude, the distance to the north or south from where you are. The Y coordinate shows your height above the bedrock. Write down the X, Y, and Z coordinates of your home in *Minecraft* before you explore. You can then use these to find your way back home after a long journey into new lands!

Every unique structure and design starts off simple. Use your imagination and a bit of planning to make your design more complex!

What other shapes and designs can you come up with using *Minecraft*'s basic unit of building?

"lines." When you plan your building in *Minecraft*, you might incorporate these and other shapes, like lines, rectangles, and circles. When you do this, you are using geometry.

The basic unit of building in *Minecraft* is the block. We can use these cubes to build 3D shapes. These shapes have height, width, and depth. Two-dimensional (2D) shapes only have height and width measurements. Adding depth to a square turns it into a cube, a rectangle into a rectangular prism, and a triangle into a pyramid. These are some of the most common shapes used to build buildings. For instance, the White House in Washington, D.C., was built using some of these shapes! Can you name a few of them?

How would you recreate the Capitol Building in *Minecraft*? What shapes would you use?

Different shapes have different features that are unique to them. Squares have four equal straight sides and four **right angles**. Rectangles have four straight sides and four right angles, where two opposite sides are longer. Triangles, which are considered to be the strongest shape, have three sides and a combination of right angles and **acute angles**. Keep the characteristics of these shapes in mind when you plan out your project. What will you build? Will you build a bridge or house? What shapes will you use?

How will you plan out your design? Will you create a 2D sketch or use a 3D modeling system?

TECHNOLOGY

Artists who use technology to create 3D art are called graphic designers. They use math to combine shapes to create complex works of art. When these shapes are put together in 3D, you can get a better look at the whole design. This process is called 3D modeling. You become a graphic designer when you build in *Minecraft*.

There are other technologies besides *Minecraft* that can help you turn your ideas into creations. Professional modelers use advanced programs to **render** 3D models before sending them to an engineer or artist to build. While you may not want to use an advanced program to create, there are apps you can use. Morphi is a 3D modeling app that turns your 2D drawings into 3D models. You can edit your drawing by making it larger or smaller or adding more shapes to make it more complex. When you are done modeling your piece, you can either share it with the app's virtual reality feature or export it to a 3D printer, laser cutter, or any other machine that can create your 3D model.

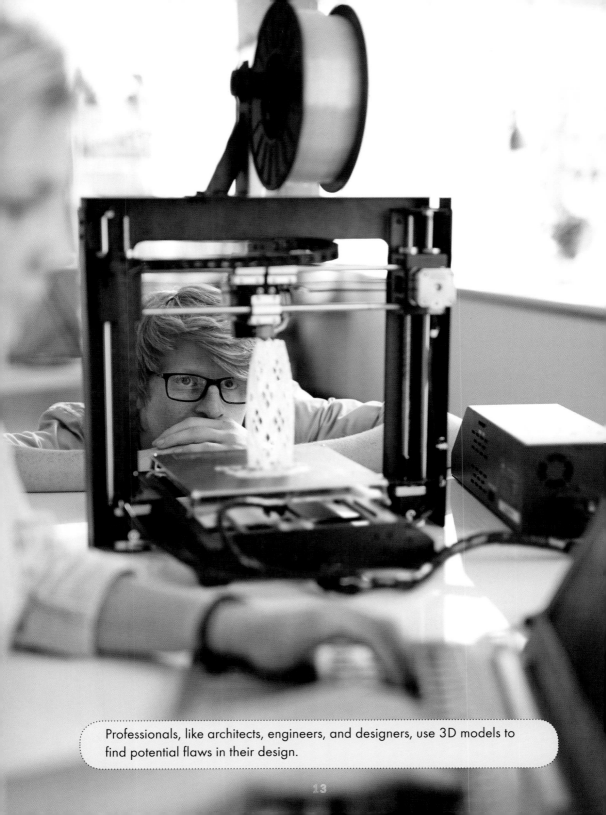

Professionals, like architects, engineers, and designers, use 3D models to find potential flaws in their design.

CHAPTER TWO

Architecture: Arches, Vaults, and Domes

Architects use geometry and other math skills in the real world. They often use reflections, translations, and rotations. A reflection mirrors a shape across a centerline. A translation moves a shape from one place to another. A rotation spins a shape around a central point. Three discoveries that illustrate these math **concepts** are the arch, the vault, and the dome. Architects use these designs to build large structures.

Arches are made using reflections. They are the same shape on both sides of their centerlines. You have probably seen arches in windows, tunnels, and bridges. One of the most famous arches in the world is the Arc de Triomf in Barcelona, Spain, built in 1888. When arches are built properly, they can hold weight above them while having open space below. For instance, the Anji Bridge in China is more than 1,400 years old and is considered the world's oldest bridge. It stands the test of

Domes can be built using a variety of materials.

Building a dome in Minecraft requires planning and patience.

time because of how well it was built—only the decorative railings have been replaced.

Arches that extend to cover a large area are called vaults. In math, when a shape is moved from one place to another, it is translated. Vaults are arches that are translated along a straight line. You may have seen a ceiling or a roof that is a vault if it is curved like an arch. The Church of Saint-Severin in Paris, France, is a great example of a vaulted ceiling.

An arch that is rotated in a circle is a dome. In math, when a shape is spun around its center, it is rotated. Domes are often used as roofs in important buildings. The roof of the United States Capitol in Washington, D.C., is a dome. What other building can you think of that has a dome for a roof?

The ancient Romans popularized the use of arches by building structures like bridges, sewer systems, amphitheaters, and palaces.

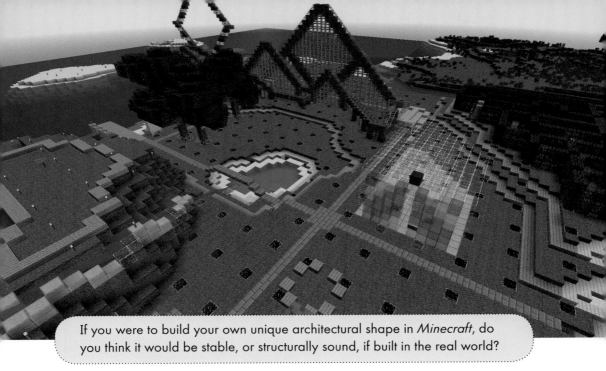

If you were to build your own unique architectural shape in *Minecraft*, do you think it would be stable, or structurally sound, if built in the real world?

The math behind arches, vaults, and domes allows designers to build very large buildings out of fewer materials. Early engineers had to worry about their buildings being too heavy. If they built structures too tall or too large, the structures would fall down because of the heavy weight. But engineers discovered that arches, vaults, and domes could bear heavier weights and were more structurally stable.

In *Minecraft*, you do not need to worry about the weight of your structures. Your buildings will stand as tall as you craft them. However, adding arches, vaults, and domes to your creations can make them look much more impressive. Instead of a small doorway, try to build a large entrance out of an arch. Instead of a flat roof on your building, try making a vault or a dome!

Try incorporating all three structures into your design.

Circles are difficult to create in *Minecraft* because the game cannot make curved lines! You must use a combination of straight and diagonal lines to create a circular shape. You can also use reflection to design a circle. First, draw a straight line. Now, create a rounded shape on one side of the straight line. Then, make the reflection of that shape on the other side of that line. Creating a shape that has two reflected sides is one way of helping to make your circle perfectly round.

ART

Some of the most beautiful and creative buildings in the world are made using combinations of arches, vaults, and domes. Architects sometimes use **symmetry** when building these structures. This means that designs match each other on both sides of a centerline. Symmetry can also help solve problems in design. For example, a roof with symmetry will let water flow down equally on both sides. Architects have to use math to design buildings with symmetry.

You can use math in *Minecraft* to design with symmetry. Your understanding of basic shapes can help you design the perfect structures. For example, if you want to design a building with double doors centered in the middle, you need to make sure that your wall is an even number of blocks in length. To create symmetry, make sure the walls on the other side are the same number of blocks in length.

Many domes feature a smaller dome-like structure at the very top called a cupola.

CHAPTER THREE

Probability: Chance in Minecraft

Minecraft uses more math than just geometry. Have you ever noticed that some items in *Minecraft* are harder to find than others, or that some items appear randomly, like seeds when you cut grass? Using math, you can figure out how often you should find rare and random items. This is called **probability**.

Probability is used in the real world all the time. Have you ever seen a meteorologist report that there was a 50 percent chance it might rain? This means that there is an equal chance of the weather being rainy or not rainy on that day. If the probability of rain were 20 percent, it would be less likely to rain. If the probability were 80 percent, it would be more likely to rain. Have you ever heard of a baseball player's batting average being .400 (40 percent)? This means that the player is likely to hit the ball 4 times for every 10 times he steps up to the plate. If the player's batting average is .300 (30 percent), then he

Try to calculate your batting average the next time you play baseball or softball!

Grass will have zero chance of dropping seeds if a block is placed on top of it.

is likely to hit the ball 3 times for every 10 times he steps up to the plate.

Probability is not a sure thing. While probability can tell you how likely something is to happen, it is not a guarantee. A baseball player who has a .400 batting average might hit the ball every time he's up to bat. Or he might not hit it at all!

You can figure out the probability of finding items in *Minecraft*. The next time you are in a field, cut 100 grass. When you do, count how many times seeds drop from the grass you cut. Take the number of seeds that dropped and divide that number by 100 (the amount of grass you cut). This will give you a probability of seeds dropping when you cut grass! You can use

Do you think probability changes as more data is collected? Why or why not?

Why do you think calculating probability is important?

this same formula to figure out the probability of getting special blocks when mining underground. Break 100 stone, dirt, or gravel blocks and count how many iron ore, gold ore, emerald ore, or diamond ore blocks appear. Divide each of those numbers by 100. This can give you a probability for each of these items and tell you how rare they are!

Even though probability does not guarantee that something will happen, you can make it more **accurate** by gathering more data. Probability uses division to figure out the chance that something will happen. If you make the denominator of your division equation bigger, the more accurate your probability will be. For example, if you calculate using 1,000 blocks instead of 100 blocks (of grass or stone or some other block), the closer your probability will be to the truth.

Extension Activity

Use geometry and probability to design a building in *Minecraft*. First, take a look at some real-life buildings you like. Try to identify specific shapes, like squares, circles, and triangles, in the design. How do these help make the building beautiful?

Next, sketch out your new building using these shapes. How can squares, circles, and triangles work together in your design to make something unique? Can triangles and circles sit on top of squares? Can triangles and squares be put together to design something new?

As you design your building, think about the idea of symmetry. How can your structure be even on both sides of a centerline? Do all buildings in the real world use symmetry? Should your entire structure in *Minecraft* use symmetry? Is there an extra-special part of your structure that should stand out from the rest?

When you build your design, think about how you used probability to show which items and blocks are rare in *Minecraft*. Can you build parts of your structure with these rare materials? Once you do, can you explain to visitors why they are thought of as rare in *Minecraft*?

What will you build next in *Minecraft*?

Find Out More

Books

Zeiger, Jennifer. *The Making of Minecraft*. Ann Arbor, MI: Cherry Lake Publishing, 2017.

Miller, John and Chris Fornell Scott. *Unofficial Minecraft STEM Lab for Kids: Family-Friendly projects for Exploring Concepts in Science, Technology, Engineering, and Math*. Beverly, MA: Quarry Books, 2018.

Websites

Science Channel—What the Ancients Knew: Roman Arch and Vault
www.sciencechannel.com/tv-shows/what-the-ancients-knew/videos/what-theancients-knew-roman-arch-vault
This video talks about how arches and vaults were important to crafting Roman buildings like the Colosseum—and why they are still important today.

YouTube—*Minecraft* Weather Forecast Machine
https://youtu.be/fTD21u0Watw
YouTuber Redstone Jazz builds a machine that predicts when it will rain in *Minecraft*. The video shows how to build such a probability machine and explains more about how probability works.

Glossary

accurate (AK-yuh-rit) something that is right or correct

acute angles (uh-KYOOT ANG-guhlz) angles that measures less than 90 degrees but are more than zero degrees

concepts (KAHN-septs) general ideas

coordinates (koh-OR-duh-nits) groups of numbers used to tell where something is

geometry (jee-AH-muh-tree) the part of math that studies lines and shapes

probability (prah-buh-BIL-ih-tee) the chance that something will happen

render (REN-dur) to make or create

right angles (RITE ANG-guhlz) angles formed by two lines that are perpendicular to each other; an angle that measures 90 degrees

spontaneously (spahn-TAY-nee-uhs-lee) doing something without planning it ahead of time

symmetry (SIM-ih-tree) the same or equal on both sides of a centerline

Index

Adam Hellebuyck is the dean of Curriculum and Assessment at University Liggett School in Grosse Pointe Woods, Michigan. Follow him on social media at @adamhellebuyck

Michael Medvinsky is the dean of Pedagogy and Innovation at University Liggett School in Grosse Pointe Woods, Michigan. Follow him on social media at @mwmedvinsky